Season of

a Lent course

by

Alison Morgan and Bill Goodman

A ReSource publication

ReSource – helping to build a church which is diverse, local, renewed in the Spirit and effective in mission.

Published by ReSource
13 Sadler Street, Wells, Somerset BA5 2RR
office@resource-arm.net
www.resource-arm.net
Charity no. 327035

ISBN 978-1-906363-13-0

Acknowledgements

Unless otherwise stated, all Bible translations are taken from the New Revised Standard Version of the Bible, Anglicized edition, copyright © 1989, 1995 by the Division of Christian Education of the National Council of the Churches of Christ in the United States of America, and are used by permission. All rights reserved.

Photos on pp 9,11,18,21,29,30,35,36,37,38,41,44,53,58,69,70 © istockphoto.com
Photos on pp 32,76 © fotolia.co.uk. Photo on p 5 © stockxpert.com
Photos on pp 20,34 © Martin Cavender
Photos on pp 15,37,42,43,51,57,64 © Alison Morgan

Printed by St Andrew's Press, Wells, Somerset.

The course authors

Ordained in 1989, Revd Bill Goodman worked in Anglican parishes in Burton-upon-Trent and Halifax for nine years. This was followed by six years in Ethiopia teaching at theological colleges in Addis Ababa. He is now on the staff of St Wilfred's, Kibworth and studying for a PhD.

Revd Dr Alison Morgan is the author of *The Wild Gospel* (Monarch 2004), co-author (with John Woolmer) of the ReSource healing course *In His Name*, and editor of *Rooted in Jesus*, an interactive discipleship course for Africa. Alison works full time for ReSource as a thinker and writer.

The Leader's Manual and accompanying Members' Coursebooks are available through our website at www.resource-arm.net, or from the ReSource office.

Contents

This Leader's Manual is accompanied by a booklet of notes and spiritual exercises for the use of each group member. These form an integral part of the course, and are reproduced in this book at the end of each session for the convenience of the course leader.

Season of Renewal : Introduction

It is commonly recognised that we are living at one of the periods of greatest change that the world has ever known. An unprecedented array of opportunities lies open before us. And yet so often this dazzling wealth of opportunity is edged with a shadow of doubt – what about our inner selves? If in terms of having and doing we are the richest people ever to have lived on earth, we are also uncomfortably aware that we are not necessarily the happiest. One journalist remarks:

Having constructed a society of unprecedented sophistication, convenience and prosperity, nobody can remember what it was supposed to be for. Just enjoying it does not seem to be enough. Indeed enjoyment as an end in itself quickly turns to ashes in the mouth. Not only is it boringly bland. It is even more boringly purposeless. There is more to human life than comfort, entertainment and the avoidance of suffering.[1]

Two thousand years ago, Jesus promised that through him we would find not just life, but abundant life. Not through the enjoyment of material wealth and a culture of opportunity, but through spiritual riches of which the world could only dream. Lent is a time in which traditionally we turn aside from the pursuit of material things, from the comfort of our modern lives, and seek to feed our souls with nourishment that is available to us only in Christ. It's a time which is often trivialised, reduced to the hopefully token giving up of this or that. And yet it's an opportunity to change gear for a while, to travel in company with one another on a different road - a less comfortable but ultimately more fulfilling road. It is our hope that this Lent course will enable you to do that, and to serve in some sense as a map for the journey.

> *The spiritual search is not for answers to intellectual questions, but for a transforming relationship with God.*
>
> Eddie Gibbs & Ian Coffey[2]

Travelling together

The course has been written according to a number of overarching principles. Firstly, it is a specifically Lent course. You may wish to use it at other times of year, but we have tried to tie it in with the calendar of the church. Secondly, we have tried to link the themes of the course with what is happening in the church and in our society, so as to build a bridge between the traditions of the church and the realities of life in the world. Lent is a time of reflection and examination, not as an end in itself but as a preparation for ministry – and in this too the life of Jesus serves as a pattern for our own.

At ReSource we believe that spiritual renewal is the key to everything we are and do, not as an event complete in itself but as part of a process which finds its natural outcome in mission. It is a pattern which occurs not once but repeatedly, beginning in the heart of each person and, like a drop landing in a pool of water from the source of life itself, continuing with an outward momentum which spreads through the church and flows out into the wider community.

We hope that this course will facilitate that momentum, and that it will act as a catalyst for growth and development in the lives not just of those who take part but in the mission and ministry of the church as a whole. We have therefore included some suggestions for how you may wish to continue your spiritual journey as individuals and as a church.

Whoever believes in me, as the Scripture has said, streams of living water will flow from within him.

John 7.38

Practicalities

The course is designed for use in small groups of 6 to 12 people, led by a group facilitator who may be the parish priest or minister, or a lay leader. It contains material for six sessions - five for the five weeks which lie between Ash Wednesday and Maundy Thursday, and one final session for the week after Easter. We hope that the final session will be one of reflection, celebration, and looking ahead, structured round a shared meal. To help link the course with the devotional patterns of the church we have included some notes on the history and meaning of Lent which the group leader may find helpful by way of background preparation. We have also included some additional notes for use where appropriate in the preparation of services for Ash Wednesday and Maundy Thursday. We hope you will find these useful if you are responsible for leading these services; but the course itself is complete without them.

Each session is designed to last for an hour and three quarters. The course material is contained in the Leader's Manual. There is an accompanying Member's coursebook containing brief notes and a pattern of spiritual exercises for each participant to follow, should they wish to do so, during the week between meetings. They should bring this booklet to the group meeting each week, as sometimes you will refer to it. We hope that you will feel free to absorb the material before the session and present it in your own words as you lead the group.

An overview

The course begins with an introductory session entitled 'Seasons of change', which offers the opportunity for course members to get to know one another, and locates the pattern of our spiritual life within the bigger pattern of creation itself. The aim of this session is that course members should begin to identify patterns in their own lives, and prepare themselves for spiritual growth in the weeks ahead.

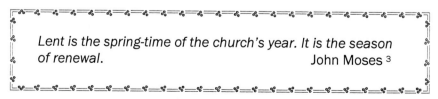

Lent is the spring-time of the church's year. It is the season of renewal.   John Moses [3]

The second session focuses on Jesus, on the twin moments of baptism and testing which preceded his active ministry on earth, and which form the basis for the traditional Lenten practices of prayer and penitence. Group members are encouraged to participate in this process, in readiness for the new spiritual growth for which they will pray in the third session. As individuals we are called to belong to one another in the church, and during the fourth week the course looks at the life and growth of the church; what does it mean to be members together of a growing vine, united by the life-giving power of the Holy Spirit? In the fifth week the group will return to the model of Jesus, for whom the period of prayer and fasting which we commemorate in Lent was a preparation for a life of active ministry. Group members will be encouraged to reflect on their own calling within the life of the community. The final session, to be held after Easter, is offered as an agape meal celebrating our participation in the kingdom of God through the risen Christ, and helping us to look forward from Easter resurrection to Pentecost mission.

We hope that participation in the course will bring about significant spiritual growth both for course members and in the life of the church of which they form part, and various suggestions are offered for how to maintain the impetus which has been created.

Endnotes
1. Clifford Longley, quoted by Roy McCloughry, *Living in the presence of the future,* IVP 2001, p.32.
2. *Church next – quantum changes in Christian ministry,* IVP 2001, p.129.
3. *The Desert - an anthology for Lent,* Canterbury Press 1997, p.xi
4. Chris Park, *Leading others into the presence of God – a worship leader's guide,* Grove 2004 p.27.

It is often said that people do not go to church because they do not believe that they are missing anything.[4]

Can we prove them wrong?

Notes for the course leader

What is Lent and how can we make the most of It?

Here is a little historical background, and some ideas which might help in encouraging people to become part of this Lent course.

Lent is a particular season

The early Christians fasted for one or two days just before Easter. This developed into a regular season of preparation for Easter, which became known in English as Lent (from the old English word for 'Spring').

Many people today sense a real need to slow down, to rethink their commitments and priorities, to make time for reflection and prayer – but somehow they never get round to it. We can offer them this particular season. It's in the calendar; the dates are already set, this course is being provided, the opportunity people long for has been arranged. Let's say to them: 'Come to the spiritual feast – all is now ready!'

Lent is a limited period

Christians have debated how long Lent should last (in particular whether to count Saturdays, Sundays and Holy Week as part of it). This is why Lent covers a longer period in the calendar of the eastern churches than in the west. But there is general agreement now on a basic model of 40 days, which echoes the 40 days Jesus spent in the desert after his baptism.

Some people in our churches will be interested in growing spiritually through a regular small group meeting. But they may be wary of joining an 'open ended' programme ('If I don't like it, how will I be able to escape from it?'). A Lent course offers a small group experience for a limited period. As leaders, we may hope it will develop into an ongoing group after Easter; but we encourage people to join by making it clear that this is a short-term commitment.

However, the limited period is also challenging. This group will not simply offer a warm, fuzzy experience; nor will it just drift aimlessly along. The aim is to allow God to change us for the better – both as individuals and together as a group or church. We seek a practical outcome by the end of this period. We look to God with eager expectation, at the same time as we look forward to the life-changing events of Easter.

Lent is for all

From earliest times, Lent has been linked with baptism. New believers were instructed and prepared during Lent for their baptism at Easter. Lent also became a season for established believers to put on the armour of God and renew their spiritual life in disciplined prayer and repentance, leading to restoration of those who had fallen into sin and to a deeper level of fellowship and spiritual growth. Many churches today invite all who have been baptised to renew their baptismal vows at Easter – a reminder to young and old that we are all in this together.

These traditions can help challenge the whole congregation to engage with Lent, and particularly with the Lent course. It's not just something for a few new members / old timers / super-spiritual oddballs ...

Lent is a gift

Some people may remember the idea of 'giving up something for Lent' – a faint and rather feeble echo of the tradition of penitence. We may prefer to challenge people to 'take up something for Lent', and particularly to take up this Lent course. Here is a gift which they can take hold of. But doing so may, of course, involve putting down something else – perhaps fasting from a favourite 'soap' or the Champions League on that particular night of the week!

A key passage for this course: John 20.19-23

During the course we shall return regularly to this text. Those who will be leading the course may like to study and pray into the passage before the course begins. As part of your preparation as leader, read the passage carefully and reflect on the points which follow:

> When it was evening on that day, the first day of the week, and the doors of the house where the disciples had met were locked for fear of the Jews, Jesus came and stood among them and said, "Peace be with you." After he said this, he showed them his hands and his side. Then the disciples rejoiced when they saw the Lord. Jesus said to them again, "Peace be with you. As the Father has sent me, so I send you." When he had said this, he breathed on them and said to them, "Receive the Holy Spirit. If you forgive the sins of any, they are forgiven them; if you retain the sins of any, they are retained."

Points for reflection

Peace to you. Jesus comes to bring wholeness, 'shalom' to those who look to him. See John 14.27-28; also the beginning of Paul's letters.

The disciples were filled with joy: the response to recognising the risen Lord is joy, as he himself predicted (16.21-22).

As the Father has sent me, so I send you. Jesus' mission will continue, through their ministry, in the power of the Holy Spirit. They do not begin their own new ministry, but continue Jesus' work.

He breathed on them. Compare Gen 2.7; Ezek 37.9-10: Jesus gives new resurrection life (spiritual life) to them.

Receive the Holy Spirit. The church is a community in which the Spirit continues the presence and ministry of Jesus, who sends the disciples out in mission just as the Father sent the Son. Those who are sent out are given the Spirit to enable them in that mission. (For more of John's teaching about the Holy Spirit, see John 3.5-8; 7.37-39; 14.15-17, 25-26; 15.26-27; 16.7-11, 12-15.)

If you forgive the sins of any, they are forgiven... compare Matt 16.19, 18.18. Continuing Jesus' mission involves declaring both salvation and judgment (see 3.17f; 12.31 – condemnation for those who side with the killers of Christ, forgiveness for those who receive his word).

Additional note on verse 22

This verse presents a difficulty of interpretation: how do we reconcile it with the giving of the Holy Spirit in Acts 2? Various suggestions have been made:

Is John ignorant of the Pentecost tradition recorded by Luke? This is very unlikely.

Is this an enacted parable, a symbolic promise of the gift which will not actually be given until later at Pentecost? (Cf 13.8: 'Unless I wash you...' points forward to a future event, the spiritual washing accomplished by Jesus' death.) Possibly.

Is this a partial bestowal only (Calvin: 'the apostles were only sprinkled with grace now, saturated with full power later')? This seems the most likely explanation (see commentaries by L Morris, H Ridderbos). Luke himself depicts the Spirit falling more than once (Acts 10.44;11.15) and several occasions when people are filled with the Spirit (Acts 4.8, 31; 9.17; 13.9). The Spirit continually manifests himself in new ways. Here in John 20.22 Jesus inaugurates the mission of the disciples and equips them for that mission; it will not actually begin until later – the day of Pentecost.

It is also possible that John is making a theological point: 'The outpouring of the Spirit on the Day of Pentecost is the act of the risen Lord!'. Easter and Pentecost should be held together (cf Peter's sermon in Acts 2.32-33).

Week 1 : Seasons of change

Welcome

20 minutes

Things you will need for this session:

- Pictures, photographs or objects to represent the 4 seasons
- Sheets of paper (A4 is a good size), glue sticks, and saucers containing lots of little pieces of paper or tissue paper in four colours, chosen to represent the four seasons (for example, yellow for spring, green for summer, brown or red for autumn, and grey for winter)
- Music chosen to represent the 4 seasons
- Course member's booklets to give out

Begin by welcoming people to the group. It is best if you establish an informal atmosphere from the start; you may want to have music playing in the background, or to offer members something to drink as they arrive.

When everyone has gathered and made themselves comfortable, invite them to introduce themselves briefly to one another. If the group has fewer than 10 members it's easiest to do this by asking them to share their name and something about themselves in turn. If there are more than 10 members you may prefer to divide them into threes.

Introducing the course

10 minutes

People may have different understandings and expectations of what this course is all about, so it will be helpful to start by giving them some background information and an overview of the things you will be doing together.

Explain that you want to begin by offering a brief summary of what we understand by the season of Lent. The main points to make are these:

- Lent is a particular season

The early Christians fasted for one or two days just before Easter. This developed into a regular season of preparation for Easter, which became known in English as Lent (from the old English word for 'Spring').

Many people today sense a real need to slow down, to rethink their commitments and priorities, to make time for reflection and prayer – but somehow they never get round to it. Lent offers an opportunity to do just that. It's in the calendar; the dates are already set, this course is being provided. Let's say to ourselves: 'Come to the spiritual feast – all is now ready!'

- Lent is a limited period

The traditional aim of Lent is to help believers rehearse the life of Jesus through their own prayers and actions, as a seasonal spiritual exercise which will draw them closer to God. It runs from Ash Wednesday, when we offer prayers of penitence and faith, to Easter Sunday, when we celebrate the new life which is ours through the death and resurrection of Jesus.

The fact that Lent is a limited period is also challenging. This group will not simply offer a warm, fuzzy experience; nor will it just drift aimlessly along. The aim is to allow God to change us for the better – both as individuals and together as a group or church. We seek a practical outcome by the end of this period. We look to God with eager expectation, at the same time as we look forward to the life-changing events of Easter.

- Lent is for all

From earliest times, Lent has been linked with baptism. New believers were instructed and prepared during Lent for their baptism at Easter. Lent also became a season for established believers to put on the armour of God and renew their spiritual life in disciplined prayer and repentance, leading to restoration of those who had fallen into sin and to a deeper level of fellowship and spiritual growth.

- Lent is a gift

Some people may remember the idea of 'giving up something for Lent' – a faint and rather feeble echo of the tradition of penitence. We may prefer to challenge people to 'take up something for Lent', and particularly to take up this Lent course. Here is a gift which they can take hold of. But doing so may, of course, involve putting down something else...

Things they need to know about the course

Explain to the group that in past centuries the observance of Lent was a collective activity based on the core elements of prayer, fasting and the giving of alms – not unlike the modern Muslim observance of Ramadam. In meeting as a group we hope to be able to encourage and strengthen one another in this way. But it's good also to make space for private prayer and reflection, so in addition to the group meeting there is a booklet of spiritual exercises for each person to do at home, if they would like to (explain that they don't have to, but they will get more out of the course if they do!).

What is the outcome we are hoping for?

The season of Lent runs for 40 days, modelled on the 40 days spent by Jesus in prayer and fasting following his baptism in the Holy Spirit. For Jesus, this period of prayer and fasting was a time of preparation for the three years of ministry which began immediately afterwards. So it is important for us to understand that taking Lent seriously may bring lasting personal change – Easter may be the end of a story, but it's also the start of a new and much bigger one. There's a lot more to Lent than giving up chocolate!

Group discussion

10 minutes

Ask people to share their experience of Lent. What comes into their minds when they hear the word? Has Lent been an important part of anyone's spiritual journey? Have they ever given anything up for Lent? What effect did that have on their spiritual lives?

Now ask them to share one hope they each have for the course. Why have they come? What are they looking to find? Is there anything they are worried about? Affirm everyone's answers, and explain that we will return to this question at the very end of the course when we look back over our time together.

Beginning with prayer

Ask someone to pray, for you as leader and for the group as a whole, that God would be with you as you travel together.

Seasons of change

15 minutes

If you can, find four pictures or photographs, or four objects which represent the four seasons. Put them on a table where everyone can see them, or prop them on a mantelpiece or against a wall.

Point out that when God made the world, he made it according to a seasonal pattern.

Ask someone to read **Genesis 1.14.**

God's relationship with the living world is governed by the seasons. Psalm 104 is a poem celebrating this.

Ask someone to read **Psalm 104.**

Ask the group why they think God chose to build this seasonal pattern into the life of the world he made?

What would it be like to live in a world with no seasons? Would it make any difference to our relationship with God?

You may get some interesting and creative answers, particularly if people have experience of living in places where the seasons are not clearly delineated. But the main thing you need to tease out is that life itself depends on the existence of the seasons – can we imagine the fulness of the autumn harvest without a preceding summer of flowers and insects, or the green  growth of spring without the cleansing cold of winter to prepare the ground?

Now point out that Jesus often taught by drawing attention to the pattern of the natural world around him. Ask them why they think this was. Was it just because that was what was there, in the same way that we tend to use illustrations from our own technological and urbanised environment?

Help them to see that there is a link between the created world and the spiritual world. When Jesus was explaining the spiritual life he chose to use stories about farmers sowing seed and getting a harvest, about nesting birds and knowing plants by their fruits, not just because these things were there in front of him, but because there is a natural affinity between the spiritual life and the life of the world around us - both are created by and depend on the same Holy Spirit. (You may like to point them to Genesis 1.2 or Psalm 104.30, both of which suggest that the physical world is 'breathed' by the Spirit of God. The words 'spirit' and 'breath' have the same root in both Hebrew and Greek).

Jesus' use of comparisons from the created world *'arises from a conviction that there is no mere analogy, but an inward affinity, between the natural order and the spiritual order'* .   CH Dodd

Why is it not rational to suppose that the corporeal and visible world should be designedly made and constituted in analogy to the more spiritual, noble, and real world?'   Jonathan Edwards [1]

Ask the group if they think the spiritual life can be seen in seasonal terms, with patterns of growth and of inactivity, with times of sowing and times of reaping?

Which is their favourite season, and why?

Now explain that Lent is a season which goes from the barrenness of winter to the new life of spring, and that you hope that for everyone in the group it will be a time of growth. Some members of the group will be in tougher places than others - for some the ground will be already ploughed and prepared for the growth to come; for others there will be a hard crust to soften, or a tangle of weeds still to be cleared. But you are confident that just as the Lord provides for the material needs of his creatures in Psalm 104, so he will provide for your spiritual needs as you meet and pray together during the coming weeks.

A practical exercise

20 minutes

Explain to the group that you would like them now to think about the pattern of their own spiritual lives, and to reflect on where they are at the moment. Different people like to reflect in different ways, so it's good to offer a choice of activities to facilitate this (the suggestions which follow can all be done at the same time). Encourage people to feel free to move around the room as they do this, and invite them to choose one of the following options:

1. Provide sheets of paper (A4 is a good size), glue sticks, and saucers containing lots of little pieces of paper or tissue paper in four colours, chosen to represent the four seasons (for example, yellow for spring, green for summer, brown or red for autumn, and grey for winter). Invite people to make a collage representing their own spiritual life as it is at the moment. Perhaps they have experienced different seasons in their relationship with God, times perhaps of blessing and fruitfulness, times of pain and dryness, times of growth and times of inactivity. Where are they at the moment? How would they represent this pictorially?

2. Play some music, chosen to stimulate thoughts of seasonal patterns, either natural ones or spiritual ones – for example, Vivaldi's *Four Seasons*, or a CD of Gregorian chant or music from Taizé to represent the liturgical seasons of the church, or a piece of contemporary music such as Green Day's 'When September Ends', or Coldplay's 'We Never Change'. Invite people to pray individually about their own relationship with God as they listen to the music. Do they recognise any kind of pattern as they look back over their spiritual lives?

3. Offer pens and paper and suggest that some people might like to write a poem or a prayer on a seasonal theme, either looking back over their lives and thinking about the different phases of them, or thinking about

17

their relationship with God and which season would best describe it at the moment.

Looking at scripture

15 minutes

After about 15 minutes invite them to go back to where they were sitting, and explain that you are going to look at a passage of scripture together, and that you will come back to what they have done after that.

Turn to **Ecclesiastes 3** and ask someone to read verses 1 to 15.

This is a well known passage. The author Ecclesiastes calls himself 'The Teacher'. He is either King Solomon, or a later writer trying to look at the world from Solomon's perspective. The whole book is a reflection on life, the way we live it and the values we hold.

Verses 1 to 8 quote a poem. It's a simple poem, reflecting on the comings and goings of our lives. We live in a framework which is given to us, a framework of time which brings different experiences and circumstances.

> *What do they notice about the pattern of the poem in the first 8 verses?*

Help them to evaluate the repetition of the phrase 'a time' – time comes, it goes, it comes again, like waves crashing on the shore of our lives - and there is nothing we can do to influence it. It's a cycle in which our lives are embedded whether we like it or not, and over which we have little or no control.

Now make sure they pick up the contrast between this repeated opening and the rest of the verse. This second part of each verse is our

part, the part where we choose our responses. Time flows ever onwards, like waves on the beach; but we have to learn when and how to ride them.

Now invite them to look at verses 9 to 15. Here the Teacher reflects on the poem. He changes the perspective from ours to God's.

What strikes them about this reflection?

Be prepared to offer your own responses to help the discussion. One obvious thing is that God wants us to enjoy our work and our time off. But the main point is that he has made us with an awareness of time and eternity so that even as we live our busy lives and cope with the things that come to us (good and bad) we will know that in everything we depend on him. It is only when we learn to see our lives in the context of God's provision and purposes that we will find contentment. The trick is to stand back, and to look at the pattern of our own experience in this broader context.

Now explain that this is what the group is all about. Tell them that it is your hope and prayer that as you together offer yourselves to God for this season of Lent, he will help you to see the bigger picture, to understand more clearly where you are in your own lives and in your relationship with him. Help the group to see that you are looking forward to this journey!

Praying for one another

15 minutes

Now say that you hope to end each meeting with a time of prayer. It may be hard for people to pray together, particularly if they are not used to informal prayer of this kind, or if they do not know one another very well. Explain that you hope they will take the risk of trusting one another, because it is as we take risks that we find blessings. If people are happy to pray but not confident to pray aloud, you might like to suggest that they pray silently but say 'Amen' aloud when they have finished, so that the others know they have prayed.

Invite them to go into threes and to share with one another the picture, poem or prayer which they have made, and then to pray for one another. The prayers they request of one another may arise out of the exercise; they may be things prompted by some other part of the evening, or they may be simply a desire that they would be able to meet with God during the week ahead.

After they have finished praying, give each person a copy of the course member's booklet and suggest that they might like to follow some of the spiritual exercises given for this week. Some people may like to do all the exercises; others may prefer to choose one or two and repeat them throughout the week - different people prefer to do things in different ways.

Ask them to make sure they bring the booklet with them next week, along with anything they would like to share from their experience of following the exercises. Make sure that you are able to share something yourself to start them off.

Endnotes
1. C H Dodd, *The Parables of the Kingdom*, London 1935; Jonathan Edwards, *Images and Shadows of Divine Things*, Yale 1948 (Edwards lived in the 18th century).

Seasons of change : exercises

Exercise 1

One of the passages of scripture we looked at was **Psalm 104**. Read it again, slowly and reflectively. Take some time today to go for a walk – even if it is only round the garden or local park. Don't try to pray; just notice the details of the world God has made. Look for the first shoots of spring, or pause to take in a flower or berry. Look at the intricacy with which it has been made. Think about its place in what we rather boringly call the ecosystem, but which in the Middle Ages they used to call the 'Great Chain of Being'. How does God provide for this insect or flower?

Now think of yourself, and the world in which you live. How does God provide for you? Thank him for his provision for you.

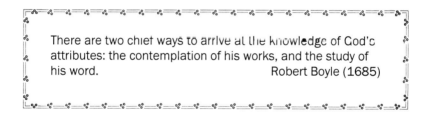

There are two chief ways to arrive at the knowledge of God's attributes: the contemplation of his works, and the study of his word. Robert Boyle (1685)

Exercise 2

We also looked at **Ecclesiastes 3.1-15**. Read it again, slowly and reflectively.

We live in a world which is dominated by time. Some of us measure its progress on our wrists, run to keep up with it, despair at the speed of its passing. Others of us watch it stretch endlessly into a future which offers little to look forward to. Some of us try and cram as much as we can into it; others of us waste it or resent it.

What is your relationship with time? Think of your time as an offering to God. Remember that a minute lasts the same length of time however you spend it. Do you know that you can stop time? Try putting little intervals of quiet into your day – a few minutes here or there, when you say 'no' to the demands around you and focus on God. Don't feel you need to pray – just think about God, and how big he is, and how he has placed eternity inside you.

Perhaps you have not too much but too little to do. God is waiting for you. Read the poem again and ask, what is this time in your life for?

He has set eternity in the hearts of men.   Ecclesiastes 3.11 NIV

Exercise 3

Read **Jeremiah 17.7-8**:

> Blessed is the man who trusts in the Lord,
> whose trust is the Lord.
> He is like a tree planted by water,
> that sends out its roots by the stream,
> and does not fear when heat comes,
> for its leaves remain green,
> and is not anxious in the year of drought,
> for it does not cease to bear fruit.

Think back to the seasons exercise in the group meeting, and use this passage to think about your relationship with God. How deep are your roots? Are your leaves green? Does your spiritual life bear fruit in the lives of others?

Now read **Psalm 1**. This Psalm uses the same image of a tree, but makes a more specific link between spiritual vitality and the way in which we choose to live. Are there any things in your life which are preventing you from accessing the life-giving water which God has made available to you? In the Bible, water is often used as an image of the Holy Spirit. Do you feel that the Holy Spirit is with you, bringing new life to you as you depend on him?

Exercise 4

Lent is traditionally a time when we mark the seriousness of our intention to focus more on God by giving something up. It works as a kind of daily reminder. As you wait for the next group meeting, begin to think about whether there is anything practical you would like to do on a daily basis in order to remind yourself that you are asking for God's blessing on your life, and that you are ready to open yourself up to him and to the other members of the group to make this possible. Perhaps you could give up a particular television programme and use the time to do these exercises? Or you might get some ideas for something which has more of an outward focus by reading **Micah 6.8**, where the prophet declares that the best offerings are not material things but behavioural ones – ways of remembering God's care and compassion for us, and passing it on to others. Can you make a daily offering to someone else in this way?

What does the Lord require of you but to do justice, and to love kindness, and to walk humbly with your God?   Micah 6.8

Exercise 5

One of the recommended lectionary readings for the second Sunday of Lent is **Psalm 27.** David was obviously finding life very difficult, and this psalm reads as a determined attempt to remind himself that he has genuinely and deliberately placed his trust God, and that this is what matters.

Read the psalm, and think about your own life. Ask yourself, are you able to pray this psalm with David, and to state that whatever may go wrong for you, you will remind yourself above all things that God is with you, and that you will experience his goodness?

Imagine yourself in God's shelter, or creeping into his tent, or standing high on a rock. Ask him to make you aware of his presence with you.

He will hide me in his shelter in the day of trouble; he will conceal me under the cover of his tent; he will set me high on a rock.   Psalm 27.5

Exercise 6

Think back over the week. What has changed for you in the course of the week? Are your hopes for the next few weeks still the same as they were in the first group meeting? Is there anything you would like to share with the other group members when you meet again?

Spend some time praying for the other members of the group, and especially for those who shared their pictures or poems with you. Ask the Lord to bless them and to draw close to them.

Pray too for the person leading the group, that he or she would know the peace of God as they prepare.

And pray for the next group meeting, that everyone would feel comfortable together, and that people would have the courage to be open with one another.

When it was evening.. Jesus came and stood among them, and said 'Peace be with you'.   John 20.21

Week 2 : Praying with Jesus

Introduction

10 minutes

Welcome everyone, particularly anyone who may be new to the group this week.

Remind the group that one of its aims is to get to know each other better. With this in mind, ask each person in turn to say their name and to say something briefly in answer to the question:

> *Is there anything you particularly remember about the place where you grew up?*

Begin with yourself. Let anyone who is new speak towards the end of this exercise.

Recap

10 minutes

Remind people briefly what is the purpose of the group, and what the theme of last week's meeting was.

Ask them how they have got on with the spiritual exercises set for the week? Did they do them all, or just one or two? Did they find them helpful? Share something from your own experience during the week.

Reflection

10 minutes

Ask everyone to think in silence about these questions:

> *Have you ever known a time in your life when you sensed the presence of God particularly strongly? What was that like? How long did it last? Were other people involved? How did it affect you at the time, and afterwards?*

Invite people to talk about this with a neighbour. Be sensitive to those who may feel they have little to offer; encourage them to share something from their spiritual journey – it does not need to be spectacular or impressive, just honest.

Looking at scripture : Jesus - like us or different from us?

20 minutes

Read **Luke 3.21-22**; then glance briefly at verses 23-38.. Involve different people in the reading, so that various voices are heard.

If your congregation follows the Common Lectionary, you may have focused on this passage about ten days earlier. If so, you could remind people of this.

In some respects, what Jesus experiences in these verses is unique, for him only. Ask the group if they can see examples of this?

Look out for and affirm answers such as:
- Jesus meeting John
- Jesus was sinless (his baptism was a sign not of repentance, but of identification with the human race, and with God's call on his life)
- The dove and voice from heaven.
- Jesus being God's Son

Don't spend more than a few minutes on this part. The point is to remind people that Jesus is unique, and that not everything he experienced is repeated in our lives.

Now ask the group :

> *In some ways, Jesus' experience is echoed in the lives and experiences of those who follow him. This includes Christians today, such as you and me. Does this passage 'ring bells' with our own experience?*

Look out for and affirm answers such as:

- Like Jesus, most of us have been baptised. Baptism is a sign of God's grace (generous love) to us, and our response to that grace.

- Like Jesus, all of us face temptation, as part of being human in a broken world. (Don't get into detail about this now, as we will focus on it shortly).

- Like Jesus, all of us need to receive God's Holy Spirit.

Ask the group what the phrase 'Holy Spirit' means to them. Look for understandings (including misconceptions), and for what they have experienced. Look for and affirm such answers as:

- The Spirit comforts us, making God's love and affirmation real to us (cf Luke 3.22).

- The Spirit challenges us by sending us into demanding situations (Luke 4.1).

- The Spirit strengthens us for God's mission in God's world (Luke 4.14).

Who is the Holy Spirit?

15 minutes

Ask the group what the phrase 'Holy Spirit' means to them. Look for understandings (including misconceptions), and for what they have experienced.

To help in this, place on a table the following objects. Explain how each one gives us a glimpse of who the Holy Spirit is and what the Holy Spirit does.

- A glass of water: the Holy Spirit refreshes and renews us, like a drink, or like a shower.
- A child's windmill – blow on it to make it spin: the Holy Spirit is invisible and powerful, like the wind that blows where it chooses.
- A small mirror – breathe on it until is goes foggy: the Holy Spirit brings the life-giving breath of God to us.
- A photo of one of your best friends (labelled with the word 'friend'): the Holy Spirit is a faithful friend who is a comfort and strength to us, who sticks by us in good times and bad.
- A photo of someone, perhaps in your family, who has been a source of guidance to you (labelled 'counsellor'): the Holy Spirit teaches and counsels those who follow Jesus.

Invite anyone who would like to do so to pick up one of these objects which 'rings bells' most strongly with their understanding and experience of the Holy Spirit. Let them talk about it, tell their story for a few minutes. Then see who wants to go next.

Help people to see that the Holy Spirit is not a thing but a **living person**, who **brings God's life-giving power** into the world.

To close this discussion, direct people back to what you have been reading in Luke 3 and 4. Highlight anything people have shared which connects with the three references to the Holy Spirit in this passage:

> The Spirit comforts us, making God's love and affirmation real to us (Luke 3.22).

> The Spirit challenges and matures us by sending us into demanding situations (Luke 4.1).

> The Spirit strengthens us for God's mission in God's world (Luke 4.14).

Group discussion : temptation

20 minutes

Ask someone to read **Luke 4.1-15.**
Explain to the group that the fact we are spiritual beings open to spiritual reality means that we are vulnerable not just to the presence of just the Holy Spirit but also to the influence of evil. This applied to

Jesus as much as it does to us.

Ask the group to look at the way the devil tempts Jesus. Divide them into small groups of about three people and ask them to identify the issue at the heart of each temptation.

After a few minutes bring them back together and ask them to share their thoughts. Look out for and affirm answers such as:

- Material provision; the temptation to try and satisfy basic physical desires when we feel the urge.
- Worldly influence; the temptation to strike a bargain with the enemy, and to worship false gods, in order to become successful in worldly terms.
- Supernatural power; the temptation to bypass faithful obedience and the suffering involved in the way of the cross.

How does Jesus respond to each of these temptations?

- Fasting and prayer.
- Using scripture (Deuteronomy 6-8) which he knows from memory.
- Keeping a clear focus on who God is, what God wants.

Many details in this passage remind us of the people of Israel in the Old Testament wandering in the desert. Help group members to see that Jesus represents God's people; he reminds them of their true calling, and how to live it out faithfully. Ask the group

> Are the temptations faced by Jesus still with us? Which of these is the strongest temptation in our culture today? Which is the strongest temptation for you personally? How can your response to temptation echo that of Jesus?

Invite people to think about these questions in silence, then to share their thoughts in their small groups.

Praying Together

20 minutes

As you turn to prayer in this and later sessions, you could light a candle and place it on a table in the middle of the room. You could also play some music for a few minutes, to lead into the time of prayer.

Reading Psalm 51

Psalm 51 is traditionally used during Lent. As a confession, read these verses from Psalm 51 together (the psalm is printed in the member's booklet so that you can be sure of using the same version). Divide into two groups, with one reading the first half of the verses, the other the second half. Invite people to offer to God the weaknesses and failings of which they may have been reminded during this session.

> Have mercy on me, O God, according to your steadfast love;
> *according to your abundant mercy blot out my transgressions.*
>
> Wash me thoroughly from my iniquity,
> *and cleanse me from my sin.*
>
> For I know my transgressions,
> *and my sin is ever before me.*
>
> Against you, you alone, have I sinned,
> *and done what is evil in your sight,*
>
> so that you are justified in your sentence
> *and blameless when you pass judgment.*
>
> Indeed, I was born guilty,
> *a sinner when my mother conceived me.*
>
> You desire truth in the inward being;
> *therefore teach me wisdom in my secret heart.*
>
> Purge me with hyssop, and I shall be clean;
> *wash me, and I shall be whiter than snow.*
>
> Let me hear joy and gladness;
> *let the bones that you have crushed rejoice.*
>
> Hide your face from my sins,
> *and blot out all my iniquities.*
>
> Create in me a clean heart, O God,
> *and put a new and right spirit within me.*
>
> Do not cast me away from your presence,
> *and do not take your holy spirit from me.*

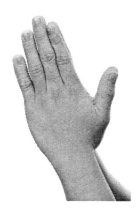

Restore to me the joy of your salvation,
and sustain in me a willing spirit.

Then I will teach transgressors your ways,
and sinners will return to you.

Deliver me from bloodshed, O God, O God of my salvation,
and my tongue will sing aloud of your deliverance.

O Lord, open my lips,
and my mouth will declare your praise.

For you have no delight in sacrifice;
if I were to give a burnt offering, you would not be pleased.

The sacrifice acceptable to God is a broken spirit;
a broken and contrite heart, O God, you will not despise.

Remind everyone that God is full of faithful love and forgiveness; that he draws near to those who are broken; that Jesus declares forgiveness of sins to those who come to him; that he truly does cleanse us and renew our spirits by the work of his Holy Spirit.

Sing a worship song together.

When you have finished, spend some time giving thanks to God, for who God is and all that God gives us. Invite people to think in silence of something or someone for whom they are thankful. This could relate to the experience they thought of earlier, the time when they sensed the presence of God particularly strongly; or to something simple and ordinary from recent days.

Then invite them to speak out their thanks and praise – perhaps just a word or a name. Encourage very short prayers, so that more people will feel confident about joining in. Start the ball rolling yourself. End this time by repeating the worship song you sang a few minutes previously.

Praying for peace

Have someone read **John 20.19-23**. Explain that this passage is a key one which we shall visit repeatedly during the course.

Read verse 19 again. Focus people's attention on Jesus' words: 'Peace be with you.' This is a greeting. The risen Lord greets his friends. Invite the group to hear Jesus' words of greeting, and respond to his friendship afresh in the silence.

The word 'peace' is rich and full of meaning in both Greek and Hebrew. Ask someone (or more than one person) to read out these words, which help us enter into that meaning more fully. Leave a silence between each group of words, during which we reflect on it, take it to heart and thank God silently for it.

- peace, harmony, tranquility
- safety, welfare, health
- prosperity, well-being
- reconciliation
- wholeness
- flourishing
- salvation

Lay a piece of paper on the floor or table with all these words written on it in a circle. Place the candle in the middle. Invite people to choose one particular word, and pray in silence for a growing experience of what it means. They should pray this initially for themselves, and then for whoever is sitting on their right and their left.

Close by saying the Lord's prayer or the grace together.

Praying with Jesus : exercises

Exercise 1

Baptism is a sign of God's grace (God's generous love) to us, and our response to that grace.

Have you been baptised? If not, why not think about it and talk to one of the leaders in your church. If you were baptised as an infant, is now the time to be confirmed?

Look at these words, which come from the baptism service in the Anglican *Common Worship.* Use them in your prayers this week, to recommit your life to Christ. Can you pray all these prayers without hesitation? If any of them seem particularly difficult to you, talk about it with a Christian friend.

In baptism, God calls us out of darkness into his marvellous light. To follow Christ means dying to sin and rising to new life with him. Therefore I ask:

Do you reject the devil and all rebellion against God?   *I reject them*

Do you renounce the deceit and corruption of evil?   *I renounce them*

Do you repent of the sins that separate us from God and neighbour?
                                                                                        I repent of them

Do you turn to Christ as Saviour?   *I turn to Christ*

Do you submit to Christ as Lord?   *I submit to Christ*

Do you come to Christ, the way, the truth and the life?   *I come to Christ*

Exercise 2

Read **Mark 1.10** and **Mark 15.38**. These verses come at the beginning and end of Jesus' ministry on earth. In both cases the Holy Spirit comes. In both cases Mark talks about the heavens being torn. In Greek the verb is 'schizo', from which we get our words 'schizophrenic' and 'schism'. It's a violent, sudden verb - as if Mark is saying that there is now a hole torn in heaven, a hole which enables us to see through into a spiritual realm previously hidden to us. What does this mean for you? Do you have experience of this hole? You may like to pray that as you seek the presence of the Holy Spirit in your life you will become increasingly as much aware of spiritual reality as you are of the

physical reality of the world around you. You may like to write a poem or draw a picture of the tearing of the heavens; or to go for a walk and look for a break in the clouds and use it as a stimulus to your prayers.

It doesn't mean that Jesus saw a little door ajar miles up in the sky. It's more as though an invisible curtain, right in front of us, was suddenly pulled back, so that instead of the trees and flowers and buildings, or in Jesus' case the river, the sandy desert and the crowds, we are standing in the presence of a different reality altogether. Tom Wright [1]

Exercise 3

Read **Luke 4.1-2.** Think about your experience of temptation. Most of us struggle with temptation in a particular area of life; for some it is money, for others anger, for others sex, or ambition, or pride... Do you know in which area the struggle is especially strong for you? Pray about that. Do you need to take some action to avoid particular temptations in that area? Do you need to talk about this with someone else?

Exercise 4

Read **Luke 4.3-14.** One of the ways in which Jesus resisted temptation was by knowing and using scripture (in this case, the book of Deuteronomy).

Do you read the Bible regularly? If not, why not start now! Read a few verses each day, and ask God to help you understand them and apply them to your life. You could start with one of the gospels. If you know a good Christian bookshop, visit it and ask about some of the Bible reading aids which are available. Maybe a Christian friend can help and advise you as well.

Have you found any particular Bible verses helpful in dealing with temptation? If so, try learning a few by heart, one each week during Lent.

Exercise 5

Read **John 20.19-23**.
Spend some time sitting quietly in a chair. Rest your hands in a comfortable position on your lap, with palms facing down. Close your eyes. Breathe slowly and deeply. As you breathe out, think of the things you wish to give to God – burdens you need to shed, anxieties which worry you, failures in your life this week. Do this until you have handed these things to him.

Now concentrate on the breathing in. Keep the same slow rhythm. But this time, breathe in God's forgiveness and love. Breathe in God's peace, which Jesus promised to his frightened and confused disciples. Remember what this Bible word means:

- peace, harmony, tranquility
- safety, welfare, health
- prosperity, well-being
- reconciliation
- wholeness
- flourishing
- salvation

Take these truths in, as you breathe in slowly and deeply. Turn your hands over so that the palms are facing upwards. Receive the Holy Spirit, who brings God's friendship and peace into your life.

Think of anyone you know who needs God's friendship and peace at the moment. Pray for them. Ask God to show you some way you might help them this week.

Endnote
1. Tom Wright, *Mark for Everyone*, SPCK 2001, p.5

Week 3 : All Things New

Introduction

10 minutes

Welcome everyone. As an 'icebreaker' ask each person to share with the group something that they enjoy doing to relax; and something that really irritates them!

Recap and Feedback

10 minutes

Summarise in a couple of sentences what happened last week. Give people the opportunity to share their experiences since then. What difference did last week's session make to their thinking and praying? Did they find any of the spiritual exercises during the week particularly helpful? Be ready to set the ball rolling by sharing something from your own experience.

Reflection

15 minutes

One of the traditional pictures of the Christian life is that of a 'pilgrimage' - a particular kind of journey.

Ask each member of the group to think back over their spiritual life so far. What have been the important parts of their journey? Has it always been smooth, or maybe sometimes a bit rough? Have there been wonderful mountain tops and also dark valleys? What about refreshing streams, or oases in the desert? Have there been key moments, important experiences? Do particular people or places come to mind?

Put out a pot of coloured pens or crayons, and give everyone a piece of paper (at least A4 size, preferably a bit bigger). Invite them to draw a picture or map of their spiritual journey so far. Encourage those who find this approach daunting to have a go, maybe surprise themselves! Make it fun.

After everyone has had a go, invite people to explain what they have drawn to the person sitting next to them. (It could be fun for the other person to guess a bit what the drawings mean before they are explained.) Encourage them to take the drawings home and complete them as one of the exercises for this week.

Sum up briefly. Everyone's picture is unique, as is their journey. But each journey has some kind of beginning; and each journey does not stand still – we move, develop, change, explore. Along the way God meets us, sometimes surprises us, encourages us to keep going. These are some of the themes of today's session in the Lent Course.

Looking at scripture : Being made new

10 minutes

Ask everyone to turn to the course booklets and turn to Week 3. They will find a list of Bible verses given in Exercise 1.

Ask three people to read **1 Peter 1.3, 2 Corinthians 5.17** and **John 3.3**.
Then ask the group:

What is this new birth or new creation which Jesus, Paul and Peter all insist on? Have you experienced this new life? If so, how has it come about: a gradual process, or a sudden crisis – or a bit of both?

Encourage two or three people to share something, beginning with yourself if no one is eager to start. Try to find and affirm two different kinds of experience within the group: someone with little church background who came to faith as a teenager or adult, and another person who grew up in a Christian family and has been walking with Jesus for as long as they can remember. Emphasise that both experiences are equally valid. Look for things they may have in common: faith, prayer, repentance, worship; the work of the Holy Spirit in our lives.

Mention that there may be some in the group who have never experienced new life. The time of prayer at the end of this session will give an opportunity to receive the gift of new life for anyone who wants to do so.

Exercise

15 minutes

Ask everyone to think about their recent experiences of 'newness'. Focus mostly on fairly 'down-to-earth' things: a new day, new job, new baby, new neighbour, new CD etc.

What is newness like? In what ways is it preferable to the old? Get them to discuss this in twos or threes.

Now ask them to think of something they 'renewed' recently. (Perhaps a TV licence or magazine subscription; or a plant they repotted.)

Ask them why they renewed it?
Look out for and affirm answers such as:

- Many things are valuable and worth holding onto.

- Some things just need a fresh chance to flourish and grow – eg a plant in fresh compost.

Group discussion

Sometimes people choose to renew their marriage vows. At Easter, some Christians have traditionally renewed their baptism vows? Does anyone in the group have experience of either of these kinds of renewal? What was the point? Was this something worth doing? Discuss as a whole group.

Looking at scripture: experiencing renewal
20 minutes

Point people again to the list of Bible verses in Exercise 1.

Ask various people to read the following verses; as they do so, ask the group to look out for what is renewed in each verse, and to say what it is after each is read.

- **Psalm 104.30** (a psalm about God's creation)
- **Psalm 51.10** (about repentance)
- **Isaiah 40.30-31**
- **Romans 12.1-2**
- **2 Corinthians 4.16**

See if the group can think of one or two other relevant verses; read those out as well.

Help people to notice the following

- Renewal is something which God does, not something we can drum up; we cannot achieve or create renewal, but instead we need to look to God and co-operate with him so that he may work in us.

- Renewal has many dimensions: it affects the whole of creation; for us humans it affects our hearts, minds, strength, ministry to others, identity... It's not just about changing the books we use in church!

- Renewal needs to be repeated – a regular pattern of life in a broken world where decay is at work.

Do we need to be renewed today? Ask this as an open question; some members of the group may not feel any need for renewal, while others may feel the need strongly. As people respond in one way or another, ask them why they feel the way they do. Encourage them to keep coming back to the Bible verses which you have read together, to hear what God's purpose and desire is.

Explore together what it means to be renewed in the various ways mentioned in the Bible. Invite people to share practical suggestions about how God brings these kinds of renewal, including examples from their own experience. Encourage them to recognize the moments of renewal which they have already experienced in their spiritual journey as refreshing oases along the way. As the journey now continues, we need to keep looking for more refreshment, so that we may continue to flourish.

If time allows, look together at **Revelation 21.1-5**. Here is a vision of the end of history: all threats and destructive forces will be removed as heaven comes to earth; the whole creation will be renewed, filled with the transforming presence of God. God will become perfectly accessible to his faithful children. This is the picture which inspires us to keep walking with God, and which draws us towards God's promised future.

Praying together

15 minutes

Ask someone to read **Lamentations 3.22-24**. Sing a worship song together, expressing praise to God for his mercy and love.

Read **John 20.19-23**. Focus especially on verse 22. Jesus' words here – 'Receive the Holy Spirit' – are in a particular Greek tense which indicates one particular event. People do not automatically have the Holy Spirit within them; they need to receive him, to welcome his presence.

In **Ephesians 5.18** Paul tells the Christians in Asia Minor to 'be filled with the Spirit.' Literally he says 'keep on being filled' – not a single event, but a regular, continuous experience. Having begun a relationship with God, we allow it to develop. We need to welcome God's refreshing presence day by day, just as plants need to be watered regularly.

Both Jesus and Paul indicate that receiving the Holy Spirit is not an experience we can manufacture, but a gift which we are invited to receive.

Stand together in quiet. Invite everyone to hold their hands out, with fists clenched and facing downwards. Ask them to think of anything they want God to take away – distractions cluttering their mind, things that worry them, sins they repent of. Encourage them to give these over to God; as you do this together, unclench your fists, to represent letting go of them, perhaps letting them fall from your hands to the floor.

Now invite everyone to hold their hands together, palms upwards. Pray aloud a simple prayer such as 'Come, Holy Spirit'. Invite everyone to echo this prayer in silence, and then to keep repeating the prayer a few times, perhaps in time with their breathing. We receive God's gift of himself, his presence, whether for the first time in our life or the hundredth time. Give thanks to God.

As this time of prayer continues, you might sing together a Taizé chant or some other simple chorus.

When Jesus says 'Receive the Holy Spirit', and when Paul says 'be filled with the Spirit', both these commands are in the plural. So this gift is not just for each of us individually, but for others, for all of us together. Invite everyone to pray in silence for the person on their right and the person on their left: that they also may be filled and renewed by the Holy Spirit. (You might express this by each person putting a hand on the shoulder of the person standing on their right.)

Feedback

10 minutes

When everyone is ready, give people an opportunity to share how they feel now. Were they aware of anything taking place within them as they prayed?

All Things New : Exercises

Exercise 1

Reflect on the following scriptures:

1 Peter 1.3 : Blessed be the God and Father of our Lord Jesus Christ! By his great mercy he has given us a new birth into a living hope through the resurrection of Jesus Christ from the dead.

2 Corinthians 5.17: So if anyone is in Christ, there is a new creation: everything old has passed away; see, everything has become new!

John 3.3 : Jesus answered him, "Very truly, I tell you, no one can see the kingdom of God without being born from above."

Psalm 104.30 : When you send forth your spirit, they are created; and you renew the face of the ground

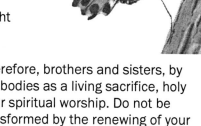

Psalm 51.10 : Create in me a clean heart, O God, and put a new and right spirit within me.

Romans 12.1-2 : I appeal to you therefore, brothers and sisters, by the mercies of God, to present your bodies as a living sacrifice, holy and acceptable to God, which is your spiritual worship. Do not be conformed to this world, but be transformed by the renewing of your minds, so that you may discern what is the will of God—what is good and acceptable and perfect.

2 Corinthians 4.16 : Even though our outer nature is wasting away, our inner nature is being renewed day by day.

Revelation 21.1-5 : Then I saw a new heaven and a new earth; for the first heaven and the first earth had passed away, and the sea was no more. And I saw the holy city, the new Jerusalem, coming down out of heaven from God, prepared as a bride adorned for her husband. And I heard a loud voice from the throne saying, "See, the home of God is among mortals. He will dwell with them as their God; they will be his peoples, and God himself will be with them; he will wipe every tear from their eyes. Death will be no more; mourning and crying and pain will be no more, for the first things have passed away." And the one who was seated on the throne said, "See, I am making all things new."

Lamentations 3.22-24 : The steadfast love of the LORD never ceases, his mercies never come to an end; they are new every morning; great is your faithfulness.

Exercise 2

One of the exercises in Week 1 asked you to go for a walk in a park or countryside. Repeat that walk this week. This time, look out for signs of renewal – buds appearing on the trees; crocuses (perhaps even daffodils) pushing upwards. Here are new leaves and flowers, which have never seen the light of day before; yet they are not totally new – they come out of the old, out of the trees and bulbs which were already there. Some bushes may have grown weaker, even died;  some bulbs may have multiplied, bringing more blooms than last year.

Pray as you walk, offering yourself to God afresh - your unique personality with all its gifts, its strengths and weaknesses and potential. Ask God to bring new growth, fresh life and beauty out of you, in order to enrich the world around you. Be open to where this may lead you; you may need to let go of some existing things in order for God to develop new life in other areas...

Exercise 3

Repeat what you did in the prayer time at the last session, when you reflected on Jesus' words 'Receive the Holy Spirit' and Paul's words 'Be filled with the Spirit.' Pray for a fresh filling today for yourself, and for the others in the group.

Exercise 4

Have another look at the drawing of your spiritual journey which you began at the last group meeting. As you look back over your life so far, invite God the Holy Spirit to retrace the journey with you. This may bring to mind other details (people, events, experiences) which you want to add to the drawing.

Give thanks to God for all that you find in your drawing.

Exercise 5

Read **Galatians 5.22-25.**

During the last group meeting, we prayed for the presence and power of the Holy Spirit to come to us as a group and individually. In his letter to the Galatians, Paul describes some of the 'fruit' of the Holy Spirit. These are the beautiful and nourishing characteristics which God wants to grow in our lives as we open up to him.

Think back to the time when you first came to know Christ, or first took your spiritual life seriously. Has the fruit of the Spirit grown in you since that time? Thank him for helping you to become more like him.

Pray that the Lord would continue his work in you. Pray for any fruit which you would particularly like to see come to maturity, or which you find particularly hard to grow. You may find it helpful to think how this fruit was manifested in the life of Jesus himself, and meditate on that.

The fruit of the Spirit is love, joy, peace, patience, kindness, generosity, faithfulness, gentleness, and self-control.

Galatians 5.22-23

Week 4 : Depending on the Holy Spirit – resourcing the church

Things you will need for this session:

- A potplant

Introduction

10 minutes

Welcome the group. As an ice-breaker, ask them to think about their experience of the church. Is there something about the church that they especially value? Ask them to share their thoughts in pairs.

You have now passed the half way point of the course, and this fourth session marks something of a gear change. Up to now the focus has been on the personal spiritual lives of the group members, following the pattern of withdrawal and prayer modelled by Jesus during his 40 days in the wilderness. But If we read Matthow chapter 4 we find that after Jesus emerged from that time, he did not go back to his old life. He started a new one. He settled in a new community in Capernaum, in the region of Galilee, and began to gather disciples and embark on public ministry (see Matthew 4.11-25).

As we continue together in the traditional Lenten practice of rehearsing the life of Jesus, we are now ready to adopt a more outward focus, and think about our relationships with the church and with the community.

Explain this to the group, and ask someone to open in prayer.

Feedback

10 minutes

Begin by giving people the opportunity to share their experiences since last week. What difference did last week's session make to their thinking and praying? How did they get on with the renewal exercises during the week? Be ready to set the ball rolling by sharing something from your own experience.

Thinking about the church

15 minutes

Explain that if we are meant to see growth and renewal in our own lives, it would seem logical to look for the same in the church.

> Ask if anyone knows what the word 'church' means? What is a church?

Allow some time for discussion, then tell them that the Greek word used for church in the New Testament just means 'the called out' – *ekklesia.* It was the normal secular Greek word for a civic assembly or public gathering. It is nothing to do with a building or a worship service, and it was used to identify a group of people called out of their usual spheres of belonging to meet together as the people of God. It's not a cosy word but a disruptive word, a word which suggests a new and alternative community gathering.

> To reinforce this point, ask them if they can guess when the first church buildings were put up?

They may be surprised to learn that it was in the third century, two hundred years after the death of Christ. The earliest we know of was built in the year 200 in Edessa.[1] We have grown used to thinking about church as what we do on Sundays in a stone building with a nice tower or spire; but the first Christians would never have thought of it that way. For them, church was about relationships, and they met together in one another's homes. Some examples you might like to look up together from the New Testament are:

- In Rome a church met in the home of Priscilla and Aquila (in Romans 16.5 Paul says greet also the church in their house).
- In his letter to the Colossians Paul sends greetings to the church that meets in Nympha's house (3.15).
- In Philippi the church met at the house of Lydia, and Paul and Silas visited them there (Acts 16.40).

46

Ask if that changes their view of church? What is this group doing now? – it's being church.

Looking at scripture : Church as vine

15 minutes

Now ask the group to turn to **John chapter 15**, and invite someone to read verses 1 to 11. In this passage Jesus is talking about what it means to belong to the church – that is, to belong to a community of people united by their relationship with him. You may like to use a pot plant as a central focus to help people think.

Invite the group to discuss this passage. Is it one they are familiar with? What do they think Jesus is getting at?

Remind them that Jesus uses illustrations from nature not just because it's what's there but because there is a natural affinity between the created world and the spiritual world. Jesus is explaining that the spiritual life they now have works in the same way that the physical life in the vine works. Help them to focus on the following two points:

- Jesus is saying that the new spiritual life which they have received through him is something which will always depend on their continued relationship with him. Just as if there is no life-giving sap in the vine, there will be no leaves or fruit on the branches, so it is with us. If we do not take care to remain in relationship with Jesus through the presence and power of the Holy Spirit, then the new life we have received will not go on to produce fruit either. We will become dry and sterile, like dead branches on a vine, fit only for burning.

- Jesus is saying that because they are all in relationship with him, they are also in relationship with one another, a relationship which is to be characterised by love and commitment. It is worth noting that most of the verbs and 'yous' in this passage are in the plural, referring to us not individually but together.

Group discussion

Now ask the group to form small groups of three people, and invite them to consider their spiritual lives in the light of this illustration. How would they rate their own personal life and growth? Do they feel like a branch of the vine which has buds, leaves or fruit, or one which is struggling to avoid becoming dry?

After a few minutes, ask them to now think about the church community as a whole. Is Jesus actively present in the lives of those who gather together to worship him each week? How strong do they feel the relationships between members of the church are? Do people know one another? Love one another?

Explain that we will pray about these things together later on, and draw them back into the big group.

Church as body

15 minutes

Give them 5 minutes to talk, then ask someone to read **1 Corinthians 12.13-21**. Here it is Paul who is trying to explain, this time to the young Christians of Corinth, what it means to be a church. He doesn't talk about buildings or institutions any more than Jesus did. Like Jesus, he uses an organic image; he compares the church to a body, made up of members who have different roles to play. He uses the same image when he writes to the Romans (Romans 12.3-5).

A practical exercise

Tell the group that you are now going to do an exercise together which will give each person confidence in their own place within the body of the church. Put them back into threes and ask them to choose one of the 3 seats they are sitting on as the 'hot seat'. They are to take it in turns to sit on this seat, and while each person is on it you would like the other two to tell them what it is that they appreciate about them. They may have known one another for years, or they may only have got to know one another over the last few weeks – it doesn't matter. What matters is that they are honest in sharing what it is that they like and respect about one another. It may help to explain that this is not an occasion for English reserve and politeness – the exercise will be of value only if they go out of their way to be real in their offerings. Point out that God loves and has chosen each person present; this should not be a difficult exercise to do.

Make sure that each person gets a go in the hot seat – you may want to help them with the timing by calling out when it is time to change over (3-5 minutes each should be adequate; you will need to be sensitive to what is taking place in each group). Be aware that once they have got over their initial embarrassment, people may find this exercise deeply moving.

After they have completed the exercise, bring them back together and ask them how they feel. Allow them to share, then ask what we learn from this exercise. Bring out two things in particular –

- that we are each appreciated for our own unique offering

- that when we express our love to one another we become much stronger as a group. Point out that this is exactly what Paul goes on to talk about in the next part of his letter to the Corinthians – whatever else we may have and do, if we are without love we are nothing.

Encourage them to look for opportunities to express their appreciation to others during the week.

The Holy Spirit in the church

20 minutes

Doing this exercise has helped each person's understanding of their own part in the body of Christ. But in using the image of the body, Paul has a more specific understanding of the part each person has to play.

Ask someone to read **1 Corinthians 12.4-11** and **27-30**.

This is one of a number of passages which list spiritual gifts and roles (the others are found in Romans 12 and Ephesians 4). For some people it may be very familiar, and they may be exercising one or more of these gifts and roles already. For others this may be new, and quite scary. Explain that just as the human body has different parts, all of which must work together for full health and effectiveness, so Paul is teaching these first Christians that we must open ourselves to the Holy Spirit who wishes to enable us to play different parts in the fellowship

49

and ministry of the church.

Start by discussing the passage in very general terms. Ask each person to look down at the different parts of their own body, and ask which part they could most easily imagine themselves using in the service of God. (You may want to do this in the whole group, or to divide people into smaller groups if you have too many for a whole group discussion.)

For example:

- tongue for teaching
- hands for healing, or practical tasks
- feet for walking alongside
- heart for caring
- arms for serving
- ears for listening

and so on.

Allow up to 5 minutes for the discussion, and then ask them if they are already doing this within the church?

Remind them of the vine illustration, and ask anyone who is aware that they are already exercising such a gift or role to share with the others in what way they feel they depend on the Holy Spirit to make this possible. Jesus promised repeatedly that when he could no longer be with them physically, he would send the Holy Spirit to live within his disciples to guide, teach and empower them (eg John 14.16-17, 25; John 15.26; John 16.12-15). Does anyone have any experience of how this works in practice? Be ready as the leader to share your own experience.

Tell the group that there is more on this topic of spiritual gifting in the course booklets. Ask them if for the moment they would like to open themselves to the Holy Spirit, to state their willingness to accept the role he has prepared for each one of them (however large or small)? Ask them too if they would like to pray for their church community, that it might increasingly become a place characterised by love in which each person has a clear understanding of the part they are called to play?

Prayer for the church

20 minutes

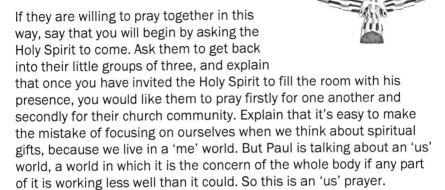

If they are willing to pray together in this way, say that you will begin by asking the Holy Spirit to come. Ask them to get back into their little groups of three, and explain that once you have invited the Holy Spirit to fill the room with his presence, you would like them to pray firstly for one another and secondly for their church community. Explain that it's easy to make the mistake of focusing on ourselves when we think about spiritual gifts, because we live in a 'me' world. But Paul is talking about an 'us' world, a world in which it is the concern of the whole body if any part of it is working less well than it could. So this is an 'us' prayer.

If they are happy with that, make sure that the prayer time is related to the group discussions you have been having by making the following suggestions.

- When they pray for one another they should remember where they felt thoy were on the vine, and what part of the body they would feel most comfortable being, and then pray that the Holy Spirit would flll and refresh each one of them, give them his gifts and show them how to exercise them in love. If they feel comfortable to do so, they may like to gently lay hands on the one being prayed for – on the shoulder, or the head.

- When they pray for the church they should thank God for the spiritual life that there is within it, and pray in whatever way seems appropriate that it and its members should grow in love, in faith and in spiritual effectiveness. Ask them particularly to remember their church leader as they pray.

Start things off by praying a simple prayer thanking God that when two or three people gather to pray in the name of Jesus, he promises to be there praying with them, and says that the Father will therefore hear and answer their prayer (Matthew 18.20). Thank God that this is possible because of the presence of the Holy Spirit. Invite the Holy Spirit to come now, to fill the room with his presence and his power, to help you all in your prayers and to give you his gifts. Then leave them to pray with and for one another.

Endnote
1. See O Chadwick, *The History of Christianity*, Phoenix 1997, p.29

Depending on the Holy Spirit : exercises

Exercise 1

A church is a gathering of people 'called out' of the world to form a new community based on a shared relationship with Jesus Christ. It is not a building, or a certain way of doing things, or a set of values; the New Testament understands a church as an organic unity of individuals come together in a new way. Jesus invites us to consider ourselves as branches of a vine; Paul as parts of a human body.

Think back to the exercise where you identified which part of the body you would most like to use in the service of others in the church. Perhaps it was

- tongue for teaching or encouraging
- hands for healing, or practical tasks
- feet for walking alongside
- heart for caring
- arms for serving
- ears for listening

Pray that God would guide you as you look for an opportunity each day this week to do this. Ask him to send his Holy Spirit to bring life to and through what you offer to others in this way. Make time to think back over the day each evening, thanking him for what you have seen him do.

For we are what he has made us, created in Christ Jesus for good works, which God prepared beforehand to be our way of life.
Ephesians 2.10

Exercise 2

The New Testament talks about the gifts of the Holy Spirit – gifts that we give, gifts that we receive, even gifts that we ourselves become. All these gifts are given to bring life to our spirits so that we may build one another up.

Gifts that we give. These are described in **Romans 12**, and are often described as 'motivational' gifts because they motivate us to different forms of ministry; they are contributions which the Holy Spirit enables us to make to the church. The ministries Paul has in mind are preaching prophetically, serving others in practical ways, teaching and explaining things, encouraging others in their faith, giving financially, providing leadership, and offering compassion.

Gifts that we receive. Paul gives examples in **1 Corinthians 12**, and (as he did to the Romans) calls them 'charismata', things given by grace. These are mostly to do with specific kinds of help that we receive from the Holy Spirit as we pray, and they are exercised primarily for the benefit of others. Paul gives as examples wisdom, receiving words of knowledge, prophecy, faith, healing, miracles, the ability to discern spirits, to pray in tongues and to interpret tongues.

Gifts that we become. These are outlined in **Ephesians 4**, and they are to do with our roles. The word 'gift' in the Greek is different here from in the other lists – it's related to the word for 'dowry'. We ourselves are given in ministry to others. The main gifts Christ gives to his church are apostles, prophets, teachers, pastors, and evangelists.

Think about the church to which you belong. What kind of gift would you like to give, receive or become in your church? Think of yourself as a present, offering what you have received to others. What's inside? It may be something very grand or it may be something very practical – remember that practical presents are often the best ones! Be ready to share your thoughts in the group next week.

Exercise 3

Read **John 15.1-11**, where Jesus compares our relationship with one another and with him to the relationship the branches of a vine have with the vine itself (you may like to look also at Psalm 80, where the psalmist likens the people of God to a vine).

Think of the coming Spring. If you are able to, you may like to paint or draw a vine or other growing plant. You may prefer to take some photographs, or to go to a garden centre and buy a young plant or some seeds you can sow. But take the time to allow the creativity of God to be mirrored in you in some way, and pray that he would fill you with the life-giving sap which rises from the roots of the vine, so that you too may produce fresh leaves and fruits.

Exercise 4

One of the passages which may be read on Sunday during this week is **John 12.1-8**, which tells how Mary poured a whole jar of expensive ointment over Jesus' feet and then, not having a towel, wiped the excess off with her hair. John remembers that the whole room was filled with the scent.

As you continue to look for opportunities to minister to others this week, remember what Mary did that day. She had reason to be grateful to Jesus – she had seen him bring her dead brother Lazarus back to life. Remind yourself what it is that you are grateful to Jesus for. He is not physically present now, so you cannot show him your gratitude as Mary did - but he did say on another occasion that what we do for others, we do for him. Think of one thing you can do today for someone else to express your gratitude to Jesus.

I'm telling the solemn truth: Whenever you did one of these things to someone overlooked or ignored, that was me – you did it to me.
                                        Matthew 25.40, The Message

Exercise 5

Read **John 20.19-23**. Pray as you prayed in exercise 5 of Week 2, sitting quietly and breathing slowly, using your hands to help you.

As you breathe out, think of the things you wish to give to God – burdens you need to shed, anxieties which worry you, failures in your life this week. Do this until you have handed these things to him.

Now concentrate on the breathing in. But this time, breathe in the peace of the Holy Spirit, the peace Jesus promised to his frightened and confused disciples. They were about to go and change the world. So are you, in your own way; for you too are part of God's plans. Breathe in slowly and deeply. Receive the Holy Spirit.

Now reflect. You have tried some new things this week. Which of them do you wish to make a permanent part of your life? Ask for his blessing and his guidance as you commit yourself to following his will.

You might like to pray this prayer written by Charles de Foucauld:

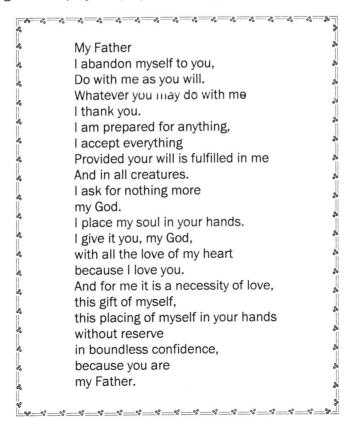

My Father
I abandon myself to you,
Do with me as you will.
Whatever you may do with me
I thank you.
I am prepared for anything,
I accept everything
Provided your will is fulfilled in me
And in all creatures.
I ask for nothing more
my God.
I place my soul in your hands.
I give it you, my God,
with all the love of my heart
because I love you.
And for me it is a necessity of love,
this gift of myself,
this placing of myself in your hands
without reserve
in boundless confidence,
because you are
my Father.

Week 5 : Made new for mission – reaching the community

Introduction

10 minutes

Welcome people to the group and allow them some time to greet one another and settle down.

Last week the group looked at what it means to be part of the body of Christ, working together in complementary ways. The exercises set for the week will have helped people reflect on what was said last week, and develop their understanding of the part they may be called to play in the life and ministry of the church.

Begin the session by inviting people to share how they have got on during the week. Did they feel any different as a result of the prayer time at the end of the last session? Remembering the 'hot seat' exercise, have they found opportunities to offer appreciation to others during the course of the week? Have they found opportunities to do specific things for others? Have they been aware of the help of the Holy Spirit? Has any of this helped them come to a clearer understanding of what God might be calling them to?

Looking at scripture : I am doing a new thing

15-25 minutes (depending on video)

Ask someone to read **Isaiah 43.18-21**, which is one of the readings for the fifth Sunday of Lent, and may have been read in church last Sunday. Explain that Isaiah, like the other Old Testament prophets, often spoke in pictures and poetry. His aim was to help people escape from the usual ways of thinking, and to imagine that things could - and would - be different in the future. This passage speaks to God's people living in exile in Babylon, struggling to maintain their identity in a society which did not share their faith. Through Isaiah, God invited them to imagine a future which would be radically different from their present reality.

Ask the group if they think that this passage offers anything to us today? Does it catch their imaginations in any way?

Help them to see that many in the church feel that we are living in just such a time of exile. Where once the church was the respected centre of every community, increasingly it is regarded as irrelevant to modern life. Where once it was felt necessary to have a Christian presence in schools, hospitals and government, Christians are now being asked to avoid offending others by talking about their faith. And yet people in our society are increasingly looking for a spiritual dimension to life in a society which for so long has been focused on material and tangible things.

Ask the group if anyone can think of any examples of times when the people of God have witnessed a spiritual renewal of the kind Isaiah describes?

Give them some examples: the Welsh revival at the beginning of the last century; the spread of the Christian faith in Russia, South Korea and China in recent times; the overwhelming national response to John Wesley in the 18th century (a period when the church had become very 'respectable' and disconnected from the needs and lives of ordinary people). If they have not seen the 'Transformations' videos which tell a number of similar stories from around the world they may like to get hold of a copy (if you have one, you could consider showing them one of the shorter stories at this point).

Ask them how they think this kind of thing happens?

Sum up the discussion by saying that it happens in two ways – one is when God does something and the other is when we do something. Normally, these things go together!

Making it work - a practical demonstration

10 minutes

Throughout scripture, water is used as a symbol of the Holy Spirit. It is the presence of water on earth which makes life possible. Isaiah talks about water bringing life to the desert. Jeremiah compares a person who trusts in God to a tree with its roots in water, living and growing even when there is drought all around. We know when we sow seeds at this time of year that it is water which will unlock the life within them.

Tell the group that you want to show them a simple visual demonstration to describe the work of the Holy Spirit. Take a bowl, as large as you have available, and fill it with water. Explain that this bowl represents your life. Take a small object such as a nut or stone, and drop it into the water. This represents the Holy Spirit coming into your life.

Ask them what happens to the surface of the water when you drop the stone into the bowl?

The answer is that ripples spread out from the central point of impact to the edge of the bowl. Explain that this is what happens as the Holy Spirit takes up residence in your life - like ripples spreading over the surface of the water, the Holy Spirit gradually brings change to one area of your life after another. You become a new creation; you put on a new identity; you receive new gifts and you grow new fruit (see 2 Cor 5.17; Ephesians 4.23; 1 Cor 12; Galatians 5.22-23).

Now ask someone to read **John 7.37-39**. Here Jesus talks about living water flowing out of each one of us.

Ask them to imagine the bowl as representing not just their own life, but the life of the church of which they are a part, and the life of the community in which that church is set. What happens?

The answer is that the ripples spread beyond each one of us and into the church; beyond the church and into the community.

Explain that that is our mission – to allow the Holy Spirit to work in us and through us, and beyond us for the benefit of those who do not yet know him.

Ask them where they think this process is meant to end?

The answer is that it ends with and in the kingdom of God. 'God is building a people for his name', Cyprian wrote in the third century – and he starts with you and with me. You may like to read them this quote, from Simon Ponsonby's book *More*:

Unless we are filled by the living waters of the Holy Spirit, which Jesus promised would flow out – not in – we will never be the blessing God intended us to be. We will never water and transform the deserts around us into life. [2]

Thinking about the community

15 minutes

Ask someone to read **Luke 19.10**. Here Jesus is explaining why he intends to stay at the house of Zacchaeus, a rich tax collector. Tax collection was a painful business at the time – the Romans used to put it out to tender, and individual tax collectors often made excessive demands on individuals and then took a cut of the proceeds. A collective grumble goes up from the crowd - why stay with *this* man, who lives comfortably at the expense of those who work day and night to earn an honest living? Jesus' response is that he came to seek out and to save those who are lost. And this man is spiritually lost.

Ask the group to think together about the community in which they live.

Who and where are the lost in that community? (Encourage them to think beyond the obvious – Zacchaeus was a man with a secure and comfortable position in society; outwardly he did not seem 'lost'). They may find it helpful to think back to the passage from Isaiah, and rephrase the question: where is the spiritual desert in the lives of those amongst whom they live?

You might like to share these statistics to stimulate the discussion:

- One third of people in the UK say they have never spoken to their next door neighbours. Is our emphasis on individual fulfilment leading us into a serious loss of community - and at what cost?

- In the period leading up to Christmas 2001, British consumers spent £35 billion - more than 9 times the gross annual domestic product of Zambia. The following year, doctors issued 22 million prescriptions for depression. Have we come to believe that money is the source of happiness, equating material prosperity with emotional wellbeing - and at what cost?

- There are more registered witches in the UK than Christian ministers. At the same time, 40% of Daily Mail readers do not know what Easter commemorates. Is it the case that our generation is on a spiritual quest, but lacks a reliable map for the journey – and what is the price they pay?

Make a note of the main things the group comes up with (you may find it useful to use a flip chart or white board if you have one). Encourage them to think broadly – focussing for example not just on the fact that there is a young offenders' institution in the locality, but rather on the needs of the young people they know.

Salt and light or dinosaurs and chameleons?

15 minutes

Remind the group that Jesus said we were to be like salt and light in our communities, making what has become tasteless tasty again, shedding light into dark places (Matthew 5.13-16). 'The Message' puts it particularly well:

Let me tell you why you are here. You're here to be salt-seasoning that brings out the God-flavours of this earth. If you lose your saltiness, how will people taste godliness? You've lost your usefulness and will end up in the garbage. Here's another way to put it: You're here to be light, bringing out the God-colours in the world. God is not a secret to be kept. We're going public with this, as public as a city on a hill. If I make you light-bearers, you don't think I'm going to hide you under a bucket, do you? I'm putting you on a light stand. Now that I've put you there on a hilltop, on a light stand – shine! Keep open house; be generous with your lives. By opening up to others, you'll prompt people to open up with God, this generous Father in heaven.

Now invite the group to consider what they think the response of the church family could or should be? You may find that it works best to divide them into smaller groups of 3 or 4 people to do this, depending on numbers. Give them 5 to 10 minutes to think about each of the following questions:

1. Do they think that salt and light are good images to describe the role of their local church within the wider community? If not, what images do they think would best describe the way we actually do relate to those outside the church? It has been suggested that in practice we tend to behave like dinosaurs, clinging to the familiar comfort of our traditions and doing things the way we've always done them; or like chameleons, striving to adapt to the new conditions and values in which we find ourselves but in the process losing our distinctive message.[3] How would they characterise their own church? What image would they choose to describe it?

2. Remembering the ways in which they think people are lost, what ways can they now think of which might help them together to be salt and light to the community? Do these relate to their conclusions last week about their own gifting and calling – in other words, are they ideas which they themselves could play a part in, rather than just things they would like to see others do?

Bring them back together and share ideas. Write them on the flip chart.

A holy priesthood

20 minutes

Summarise the discussion by asking someone to read **1 Peter 2.4-10**. Taking inspiration from Psalm 118 and Jesus' own words (Matthew 21.42), here Peter gives a picture of the church as a building made not of bricks and mortar but of living stones, people of flesh and blood. We know that Peter was given his name by Jesus (he was previously known as Simon) because the name Peter means 'rock', and Simon was the rock on whom Jesus promised to build his church (Matthew 16.18). So perhaps Peter was remembering that image too as he here describes individual Christians as the building blocks of the church.

Remind them that the word 'church' means the gathering of those who are 'called out' of the world. In this passage Peter shows that he is aware that we are called out of the world not so that we may seek refuge together somewhere else, but so that we may minister the love of God back into it – so that we may become priests to our communities. And he knew, because Jesus had told him when he gave him his new name, that this in turn is the means by which the kingdom of God is built both on earth and in heaven.

Over the last few weeks the group has looked at their own life as living stones, at the life of the church as a spiritual house, and now today at their collective calling as priests to the community. After Easter you will meet again for the last time. So take a little time now to reflect briefly on your journey together, and to begin to think about the way ahead. Invite the members of the group to spend some time during Holy Week thinking about what they have learnt and any ways in which they feel they have changed, and say that there will be an opportunity to talk about this when you meet in a couple of weeks' time for a shared meal.

There is one further thing to discuss together. What would they like to happen next? Do they feel the course has been complete in itself, or would they like to find some way of building on what has been achieved? Spend a few minutes brainstorming together, and say that this is something you can discuss again when you meet for the meal.

Some possibilities may be:

- To continue as a group, following some material such as Michael Mitton's 'Saints at Prayer' course or ReSource's discipleship course
- To run an Alpha course together, or to hold some social events or discussion evenings for non church-going friends
- To share with the church as a whole what they have been doing, with the aim of encouraging their brothers and sisters in Christ to join them in looking for new ways of doing things – one way is to use the 'Growing Healthy Churches' material available from ReSource
- To look for a means of growing together – for example holding a church weekend away on a topic to do with renewal for mission
- To offer to present some thoughts to the PCC – most churches will be forming a new church council at this time of year – with a view to stimulating further discussion

A time of prayer

10 minutes

Put people back into groups of 3 or 4, and ask them to pray together. From Ash Wednesday to today they have been on a journey with Jesus. They have followed his example, absorbed his teaching, and claimed the promise of the Holy Spirit. Now Easter is approaching, when we remember together his death and resurrection to new life. Invite them to share any particular needs or requests with one another, and then to pray for one another in turn that the coming Holy Week would be a special time, a time in which they would be drawn closer to Jesus.

In conclusion

Some people find it easy to think visually and practically. Buy a tub of air-drying modelling clay (available from craft and toy shops) and give each person a lump to take home in a plastic bag. Invite them to make a model to represent anything which has inspired them as they have worked through the course. It could be something based on one of the illustrations, like the vine; something based on one of the exercises you have done together; something representing their vision of the future; something relating to their own prayer times as they have worked through the weekly exercises. Encourage them to bring it to the shared meal.

End the session by choosing a date and place to meet again after Easter. This last session will be a time to relax and celebrate together, to share a meal, and to look ahead. You could meet in the home of one of the group members; perhaps each person could make a contribution to the meal.

Come to him, a living stone, though rejected by mortals yet chosen and precious in God's sight, and like living stones, let yourselves be built into a spiritual house, to be a holy priesthood, to offer spiritual sacrifices acceptable to God through Jesus Christ.

1 Peter 2.4-5.

Endnotes

1. Distributed by Gateway Christian Media, www.gatewaymedia.org.uk
2. Simon Ponsonby: *More - How you can have more of the Holy Spirit when you already have everything in Christ* (Victor 2004), p.19.
3. See Alison Morgan, *The Wild Gospel*, Monarch 2004, chapter 6.

Week 5 : Made new for mission

Exercise 1

Read **1 Peter 2.4-10**. Think back over the last few weeks. What difference has the course made to your thinking and praying? How have things changed for you? Were there any key moments, either in the group meetings themselves or as you have worked through the weekly exercises at home? Do you feel that you are truly a living stone? Make a note here of the three things you most wish to carry forward with you:

1.

2.

3.

Exercise 2

Look at **Psalm 118**, which contains the verses Peter was referring to and which is set as a reading for Palm Sunday. Thank God for sending Jesus and for making him the key stone in a new spiritual structure.

Now think again of **1 Peter 2**. What is your vision for the church as a spiritual house? Spend some time praying, and asking God to show you his hopes for your church. Make a note below of anything which comes to mind.

Exercise 3

Read **Luke 19.28-40,** which tells the story
of Jesus' entry into Jerusalem.
Jesus was riding into a city which he knew
would welcome him only superficially. He
knew that it was a place where God would
not be recognised or honoured, and yet he
was prepared to go there.

Now read **John 20.21**: 'As the Father has sent me, I am sending you'.
Think of the community in which you live. Are you prepared to be sent
like Jesus, to ride out like him from your safe places and take risks in
order to make God known in your community? How can you and the
church to which you belong minister as a holy priesthood to this
community?

Try and think of one practical thing you can do this week to minister in
some way to someone who does not know God. One thing, perhaps,
that you could imagine Jesus doing.

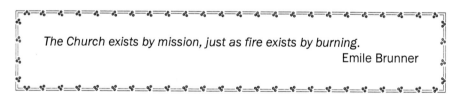

The Church exists by mission, just as fire exists by burning.
Emile Brunner

Exercise 4

(This exercise is best done on Maundy Thursday).

Read **John 13.1-17,** which is the passage set for today. Washing
someone's feet after a day's walking was the most practical thing you
could do for them to demonstrate respect and concern. Sometimes
we do it today as a spiritual exercise, but it can feel rather odd to
remove the comfortable shoes and socks which keep our feet clean in
order to do something we don't normally do for one another.

Can you think of a more effective way to wash someone's feet for them today, a way of doing something practical to make their journey through life a little easier?

Exercise 5

Read **Matthew 13.1-23**, which tells the story of the farmer sowing his seed.

Often we find that as we share our experience of what it means to be made new and to grow in Christ, people will rebuff us. Some, however, will not. Are you willing, like the farmer, to sow your seeds anyway?

Exercise 6

Using the clay which was given to you at the last meeting, make a model to represent anything which has inspired you as you have worked through the course. It could be something based on one of the illustrations, like the vine; something based on one of the exercises you have done together; something representing your vision of the future; something relating to your own prayer times as you have worked through the weekly exercises, or just a representation of who you are and where you are going. Take your model to the shared meal so that you may all encourage one another.

The Holy Spirit did not come for our entertainment or excitement. He filled the church so that the church might fill the world.
Simon Ponsonby

Week 6 : Celebrating the kingdom

Introduction

This final session of the Lent course is planned as a time of thanks and celebration, and should take place in the week following Easter or, if preferred, the week after that. The aim is to look back over the course, to share and reflect together on your experiences, and to draw the threads together as you celebrate the death and resurrection of Jesus. We hope that you will want to look to the future too; to thank God for the gift of his Holy Spirit, and to respond to his calling on your lives.

The evening is structured around a shared meal. You may wish to play some background music to centre people in Christ – a CD of songs from Taizé or Gregorian chant, some worship music, or perhaps the seasonal music which you listened to in Week 1.

Begin by welcoming people and receiving their gifts of food. If they have brought something they have made from the clay given out at the last session, invite them to place it on a table.

John 20.19-23

Invite everyone to sit down, and open the evening by asking someone to read **John 20.19-23**, the key passage for the course (you may wish to read again the notes on pp 9-10).

Invite them to focus on the various elements of this passage:

Peace be with you. These are the words with which Jesus greeted the
disciples when he met with them on the day of his resurrection. Say these
words aloud together now, then allow a few minutes for people to greet
one another informally and catch up on their news. Then pray together
that the peace of Jesus would rest upon you all. Remind them of the
prayer for peace in Week 2, and give them the opportunity to share any
ways in which they feel they have received peace from God over the last
few weeks.

As the Father has sent me, so I have sent you. Remind them that at various points during the course, and most particularly in the last session, you have looked together at what this 'sending' might mean for each one of you. Give people a chance to say how they feel about that now that the course is over. What difference is taking the course going to make to their lives?

Receive the Holy Spirit. Ask people to think back to Week 3 when you prayed together for the Holy Spirit. Looking back now, has this prayer or the exercises which followed it changed them in any way? What is that going to mean in practice?

If you forgive the sins of any, they are forgiven... This is a startling verse, but it is clearly a call to ministry. The benefits we receive in Christ are not benefits for us alone; they are to be shared. We are sent to minister to others. What are the implications of this for your church as it relates to the community?

A shared meal

Invite someone to read **1 Corinthians 11.23-26.** Remain silent together for a short time, thanking God in your hearts for the gift of life which he has given to us through Jesus.

Enjoy your meal!

Looking ahead

After the meal, while coffee is being served, would be a good time to relax and look together at the clay models people have made. Ask each person to explain their model to the others. Remind them that in the first week you said we would reflect at the end on what we have received. Has the course lived up to their expectations?

When you have done this, remind people that in the last session you began to think of the best way to carry forward what you have learnt and received together over the last few weeks. Possibilities suggested included:

- To continue as a group, following some material such as Michael Mitton's 'Saints at Prayer' course or ReSource's discipleship course
- To run an Alpha course together, or to hold some social events or discussion evenings for non church-going friends
- To share with the church as a whole what they have been doing, with the aim of encouraging their brothers and sisters in Christ to join them in looking for new ways of doing things – one way is to use the 'Growing Healthy Churches' material available through ReSource
- To look for a means of growing together – for example holding a church weekend away on a topic to do with renewal for mission
- To offer to present some thoughts to the church council – most churches will be forming a new church council at this time of year – with a view to stimulating further discussion

What thoughts do people have now? Spend some time thinking this through.

A time of praise and prayer

After you have done this, move into a time of worship, singing together or listening to a worship CD.
Finally, spend some time praying for one another and for any future plans you may have as individuals, as a group or as a church.

Ideas for an Ash Wednesday Service

We hope that the notes which follow will be of use to you if you are planning or leading an Ash Wednesday service.

The Worship Service

We can use liturgy and the traditions of Lent creatively, to meet the needs of the people we serve.

Some people's lives are full of rushing around. A service which offers stillness can be a blessing.

Some people's lives are full of clutter, particularly possessions. A plain, uncluttered worship environment can be a blessing.

Some people's lives are full of words which bombard them at every turn. Periods of silence can be a welcome relief. (Brief guidelines about how to use the silence may also help those who are not used to silcnoo.)

Some people's lives are isolated and lonely. Worship together can give a sense of community, being part of other people. This could include neighbouring churches (a joint service for Ash Wednesday?), and the church in the wider world.

Some people live adrift in the present, with little sense of what has gone before and little vision for what is to come. Traditions such as the practice of Lent can help people connect with the past, give a sense of being part of something which has stood the test of time; this can also help give hope and direction towards the future.

The Sermon

One of the passages set for Ash Wednesday in the Anglican *Common Worship* lectionary is **Luke 15.11-32.** Here are some suggestions about how you might use that famous story. (Note that in Year C the same passage is also set for the fourth Sunday in Lent. So unless you wish to focus on this rich story on both occasions, you may prefer to choose a different passage for Ash Wednesday, perhaps focusing the sermon on the key text for the course, **John 20.19-23.** See notes on p.9).

Enter into the story which Jesus told. Use careful study of the passage, and also creative imagination, as you picture the scene and enter the world of the text.

You could focus on some **key moments** in the story:

Give me my share of the property (v12). An unusual and presumptuous request; inheritance usually came after the death of the father. It's as if this son is saying to his father: 'I wish you were dead'!

I will set out and go back (v18). The turning point; the younger son's change of direction leads to a total change in his situation and status.

He ran and put his arms around him...(v20). The outrageous behaviour of the father: he runs, and embraces the son who has shamed him, giving him honourable restoration to the family - in public!

Father, I have sinned...(v21). The young son shows genuine repentance; but his prepared speech is cut short by the overflowing compassion and generosity of the father. Did the son expect this?

He became angry and refused to go in (v28). The older son refuses to eat with his family, and rejects his responsibilities at the feast which his family is hosting. He too shames his father. He does not address his father, and refers to his brother as *this son of yours. For all these years I have been working like a slave for you* suggests a growing resentment.

His father came out and began to plead with him (v28). Again the father is willing to dishonour himself in public. He calls him *son* (cf 15.24). The father loves this son just as much as the younger one; *all that is mine is yours* (cf 15.12). The elder son is unaware of the father's generosity to him.

You killed the fatted calf for him (v30). Why should sin be rewarded with a generous welcome? God's grace and mercy offends our sense of what is 'right' and 'fair' (cf Matt 20.1-16).

Encourage people to examine themselves and **think about their own lives in terms of this story**.

Where are they now on your spiritual journey? Do they identify particularly with one of the three major characters in this story? Help them to find their place in the story:

> **The younger son?** Are you running away from God? Enjoying living far away? Sensing your need of your heavenly Father? Turning round? On your way home? In the arms of the Father? Experiencing and celebrating the Father's lavish generosity?

> **The older son?** Are you working hard, trying to do what is right? Shocked at your Father's generosity? Angry, resentful at the attention given to others? Jealous of those who have done what you never did? Unwilling to celebrate when others receive God's favour? Unaware or forgetful of all the good things God gives you each day?

> **The father?** Are you becoming more like your heavenly Father? Feeling his grief as he looks on a rebellious and broken world? Willing to forgive from the heart? Looking out for the lost? Reaching out with hands of compassion to the broken? Learning to give generously to all? Wanting to celebrate joyfully when you see good things?

(for further reading see Henri Nouwen's classic book, *The Return of the Prodigal Son*, DLT, 1994)

The parable is left open-ended. Will the elder brother let go of his resentment and self-righteousness, and go in to join the celebration? Will the Pharisees and scribes change, and join the 'sinners' at Christ's table?

We need to 'finish the story', one way or another – by the response we make in our own lives!

Ideas for a Maundy Thursday Service

During Holy Week, the Common Worship Lectionary provides selected readings from John's gospel and Luke's gospel. Here are some ideas based on those readings.

As illustrations for the sermon, why not weave in a couple of the stories and insights which were shared during sessions of the Lent Group – about creation, prayer, temptation, renewal, community, mission? (You might like to check this out with the relevant group members if it involves mentioning names.) You could also bring into the service a particular time of prayer using something from one of the Lent Group prayer times or exercises.

Either

Luke 22.7-27

Read the passage, looking particularly at verses 19-20.

Focus on who Jesus is and what Jesus does

Jesus takes something familiar – the Passover meal – and explains it in a new way. He develops the meaning of traditional Passover images into an understanding of his death and the kingdom.

He took a loaf of bread... Instead of pointing to the historic deliverance of Israel in the past (Passover), Jesus looks ahead to his own death and vindication. Rather than saying, 'This is the bread of affliction', as expected in the Passover meal, he says *This is my body, which is given for you.* He is indicating that God is bringing liberation, a new 'exodus'; this is to be found in Jesus himself, especially in his body, broken on the cross.

Focus on ourselves

Do this in remembrance of me. What does it mean for Jesus' followers – then and now – to 'remember' him? In biblical thought, recalling the past leads on to making a response – to action, which brings real benefit in the present and future. A meal in memory of Jesus should celebrate and prolong his attitudes and lifestyle, embodying these things in the lives of the community who choose to remember him.

Focus on our relationship with God

New covenant in my blood. Covenant indicates a relationship of faithfulness and love between God and humankind. Blood implies 'life' (see Leviticus 17.14), which is poured out in death.

See Jeremiah 31.31-34, which emphasizes forgiveness of sins at the heart of this new covenant. (You could also look at Exodus 24.3-8, where the 'blood of the covenant' is sprinkled on people and altar.)

Explore this key idea of how God has made it possible for us to have a relationship with Him.

Or

John 13.1-17; 31b-35

The foot washing incident is a display of Jesus' love (13.1); a symbol of saving cleansing (13.6-9); and a model of conduct which disciples must follow (13.12-17).

Jesus, knowing that the Father had given all things into his hands, might be expected to produce a sign of great power; instead he *took off his outer clothing...began to wash his disciples' feet.* Jesus produces an act of humility, even towards his betrayer, which shatters the disciples' sense of what is socially fitting. (The disciples would perhaps have been happy to wash Jesus' feet, but not to wash each others' feet, since this was the task of the lowliest servant. For their master to wash their feet was unthinkable.) This action is a sign of his coming death, which will be an equally shocking and bewildering act of self-denying love. The disciples cannot yet understand how Jesus must go to the cross, so they cannot understand this symbolic act which anticipates it.

I give you a new commandment, that you love one another. Just as I have loved you, you also should love one another. Here is a pattern repeated throughout scripture: God's love is revealed to people and experienced by them; nourished by that love, they become grateful, and respond by learning how to give love in return. The word used for love here is 'agape' – the highest form of self-giving love, which comes from God. We need first to receive it, and then to learn to share it with others.

The command to love is not really new: Jesus and his friends know well the words of Leviticus 19.18 and especially Deuteronomy 6.4, which call the faithful to love God and their neighbour. But Jesus takes the old and renews it, taking it to a new dimension. By his own actions, Jesus gives his followers a model of what love involves: they are to wash each other's feet (13.14-17), and to give their lives in love for others (13.35, 15.13). The fellowship of those made clean by Jesus must be characterized by this kind of humble, selfless, sacrificial love.

What might it mean for us today?